THE SLAVE WARS

FOR KIDS

THE SLAVE WARS

A Fascinating Look At The Brave People Who Fought To Overthrow The Tyranny Of Slavery

FOR KIDS

CHARLES MCKINNEY

The Slave War

A Fascinating Look At The Brave People Who Fought To

Overthrow The Tyranny Of Slavery for Kids

Copyright © 2023 by Dr. History

TABLE OF CONTENTS

INTRODUCTION

"There is no record of any previous instance in history where slaves rose against their masters in such numbers, and possessed themselves of arms with such success."

- Appian, The Civil Wars (Book 1.116)

In this discussion on Slave Wars, we will explore how enslaved people fought against their enslavement at great personal cost. Whether they reacted with individual rebellious acts or mobilized large-scale uprisings, the impact of these actions eventually brought a legal end to the institution of slavery. By analyzing factual primary and anecdotal secondary sources, we will understand the historical context for these wars, the desperate desires of the enslaved people to emancipate themselves, and the historical legacy of their choices.

I am sure we all ask why people throughout history have thought they had a right to enslave others. It seems quite unthinkable to the modern liberal society that such atrocities occurred legally.

The justifications for enslaving others are complicated and diverse and differ considerably depending on the period of history, the geographical location, and the culture of the people in question. Some broad social and historical factors contributing to the practice of slavery include the following:

Economic reasons: Enslaving people was frequently seen as a means to acquire cheap labor for labor-intensive jobs like mining, agriculture, and domestic work. Enslaved people had to work long hours in brutal circumstances without wages or basic human rights, which allowed those who owned them to achieve high profits from their labor.

War and conquest: Throughout history, enslavement governed populations defeated in war and conquered rival groups. People seized during raids and wars were frequently sold into slavery or compelled to work for those who captured them.

Ethnic and racial prejudices: In many nations, nations that were deemed inferior or different due to their race, nationality, or religion were often enslaved. This was frequently justified by an assumption that the people enslaving them were superior to them.

Hierarchy and social status: In some civilizations, enslaved people were seen as belonging to a lower class or even being subhuman and were deemed to be property, not people.

Traditional or cultural norms: In some societies, slavery was a traditional practice that was assumed to be normal and necessary for the functioning of society. This idea was often strengthened by cultural beliefs and traditions justifying the practice.

Let's look at the brave men and women who denied these premises and fought for freedom.

INTRODUCTION TO SLAVE WARS

The Zanj Rebellion of 869-883 AD. This major uprising in Iraq against the Arab Abbasid Caliphate by enslaved Africans. The Zanj (Tanzanian) slaves revolted against their Arab rulers, led by Ali bin Muhammad. They succeeded in capturing the city of Basra and other big towns, and formed their own nation, called the "State of the Blacks." In the end, they were defeated but they had ten successful years of freedom.

Slave wars seems an unlikely term to use as a header for this discussion. Slaves or enslaved people, the correct term to use nowadays, are usually described as "defeated" and "fearful" and are seen as trying to remain invisible and keep out of trouble with those who own them. Nonetheless, the term "slave wars" means just that. It's a series of rebellions and uprisings throughout history by enslaved people seeking to free themselves from their oppressors. In desperation, they were forced into brutal and violent conflict. There were seldom happy endings, but the rebellion paid off in the long run, and the terrible scourge of slavery was abolished bit by bit.

Throughout human history, people have enslaved and abused other people, and enslaved people have thrown off their fears, and their inherent human instinct to survive and embarked on a fight for freedom. Slave wars played a critical role in the fight for the equality and freedom of enslaved people. These wars have also significantly contributed to the broad and ongoing struggle for social justice and human rights worldwide.

Notable Slave Wars throughout History

Let's briefly examine some notable Slave wars throughout history. Many of these have been immortalized in literature, movies, or series and certainly make viewing fascinating.

In order of their occurrence were;

The Third Servile War occurred between 73-71 BC. This was made famous by the rebellious slave Spartacus who led a dramatic, albeit unsuccessful, rebellion against Rome known as the Gladiator War.

The Zanj Rebellion of 869-883 AD. This major uprising in Iraq against the Arab Abbasid Caliphate by enslaved Africans. The Zanj (Tanzanian) slaves revolted against their Arab rulers, led by Ali bin Muhammad. They captured the city of Basra and other big towns and formed their own nation called the "State of the Blacks." Ultimately, they were defeated but had ten successful years of freedom.

The Stono Rebellion of 1739 occurred in South Carolina and was the biggest uprising in the British colonies before the American Revolution

First Maroon War (1739-1740)

The Maroon Wars were a procession of confrontations that occurred in the 17th and 18th centuries in the Caribbean between enslaved Africans and their European Colonizers. The slaves who escaped their captors formed independent colonies in remote and unreachable areas such as mountains, forests, or swamps. They developed their own language and society and raided nearby ranches for supplies.

The most famous Maroon Wars were the First Maroon War

in Jamaica from 1728-1739 and the Second Maroon War in Jamaica from 1795-1796. In both cases, the Maroons negotiated peace treaties with British authorities, granting them some autonomy.

The rebellion of Túpac Amaru II from 1780-1783 was a rebellion in Peru led by indigenous leader Túpac Amaru II. Enslaved people were included among its participants.

The Haitian Revolution, which occurred in Haiti between 1791-1804, was a successful slave revolt that allowed the establishment of the first autonomous black country in the Western World. This conflict was incited by enslaved Africans who rioted against their French colonial masters.

The Igbo Landing of 1803 was an act of mass resistance by Igbo slaves in Georgia, USA. The slaves opted to walk into the water and drown rather than be enslaved.

The German Coast Uprising of 1811 was a slave rebellion in Louisiana led by Charles Deslondes, a slave driver of African heritage.

A Slave revolt in Barbados in 1816 was a slave uprising in the

British colony of Barbados.

Nat Turner's Rebellion of 1831 was an unsuccessful slave rebellion led by a man called Nat Turner in Virginia. This rebellion caused the deaths of at least 60 white people. Nat Turner was an enslaved African-American pastor.

The Malê Revolt of 1835 was a Muslim slave rebellion in Brazil, led by West African Muslim slaves from present-day Senegal.

Enslaved Africans caused the Amistad Rebellion of 1839 when they rose against their oppressors on the Spanish slave ship La Amistad. This resulted in a dramatic landmark court case in the US, which we'll discuss later.

The Seminole Wars of 1816-1858 were a sequel of conflicts between the US government and the Seminole Native American tribe in Florida. It involved Seminole opposition to the forced eviction of escaped slaves who had become part of their social structure.

The Cuban Slave Revolt of 1843 was a failed slave revolution in Cuba led by José Antonio Aponte, an Afro-Cuban. The rebellion was held against the Spanish colonial authorities.

The Gullah Wars from 1811-1858 were a series of rebellions by Gullah people, African Americans who resided in the Lowcountry region of the southeastern U.S.

The Indian Ocean slave trade rebellions in18th and 19th centuries were a series of uprisings by enslaved people on ships that were engaged in the Indian Ocean slave trade.

There were, of course, many other minor slave rebellions and individual acts of defiance. We have chosen more significant ones and will look at some in more detail.

Fun Fact:

An interesting fact about the Gullah Wars is that the Gullah people successfully resisted and weakened the system of slavery in several ways, including through their use of religious practices and cultural beliefs. The Gullah people believed in the energy behind "rootwork" or "conjuring," which included using herbs, amulets, and other metaphysical means to protect themselves from hurt and curse their overlords.

Fun Fact:

A rather gruesome fact about the Cuban Slave revolt was the extreme violence with which the Spanish colonial authorities suppressed it. They carried out extensive torture, executions, and other cruelties against the enslaved and free people of African descent and were thus suspected of being involved in the rebellion. This repression gave Cuba the reputation for being one of the severest slave societies in the Americas.

Replace the missing words.

The Zanj -1- of 869-883 -2-. This major uprising in -3- against the Arab Abbasid Caliphate by enslaved Africans. The Zanj -4- slaves revolted against their -5- rulers, led by Ali bin Muhammad. They succeeded in -6- the city of Basra and other big towns, and formed their own -7-, called the "State of the -8-." Ultimately, they were -9- but had ten successful years of -10-.

Answers:

1. Rebellion
2. AD
3. Iraq
4. Tanzanian
5. Arab
6. Capturing
7. Nation
8. Blacks
9. Defeated
10. Freedom

DEFINITION OF SLAVERY AND ITS HISTORY

Slavery, as we all know, is a system now banned worldwide in its original form, in which people are dealt with as property and are compelled to work for poor provisions and shelter and no pay. They are usually purchased and sold as if they were commodities and have no control over their lives, their bodies, or how they use their labor. Slavery has occurred in numerous forms throughout human history and does exist in some areas of the world, even today, although not in its original form.

The history of slavery can be traced back to ancient peoples, such as Greece, Mesopotamia, and Egypt, where slaves were often seized in war or acquired from other regions. In Ancient Rome, slaves were used for labor, particularly construction, mining, and agriculture. In Ancient Egypt, enslaved people built the pyramids, and Herod the Great used slaves to carry water through the desert and up the mountain to Masada.

During the transatlantic slave trade, which endured from the 16th to the 19th century, millions of Africans were forced into ships and carried to the Americas. They were traded as slaves to work on sugar, tobacco, and cotton plantations. The need for cheap labor steered this trade.

The practice of slavery was abolished in most countries during the 1800s, with the British Empire taking a prominent position as abolitionists, which is quite strange when one recalls their intense involvement as colonial oppressors. Slavery continued to occur in other parts of the world, including the U S, where it was not completely abolished until the conclusion of the Civil War in 1865.

Even today, slavery remains an issue in many countries, with about 21 million people living in some type of slavery or forced labor situation worldwide. Endeavors to combat slavery are a combination of legal measures, such as legislation against human trafficking, and advocacy and campaigns which raise awareness.

An interesting example of modern-day slavery is human

trafficking. This is very across Asia, Africa, and third-world economies.

Human trafficking refers to the illicit and exploitative marketing of human beings for various nefarious intentions. These include sexual exploitation, forced labor, and sexual and even organ harvesting.

Here are some examples of human trafficking:

Forced labor: During forced labor, a person is conscripted, transported, or entrapped for the goal of forced labor. A person, for example, might be guaranteed a job in a foreign country, but upon their arrival, they are compelled to work under inhumane circumstances and for little or no pay. Sometimes they are locked into factories or buildings under very unsafe conditions.

Sexual exploitation: A person, usually a young girl or a less often but still frequently young boy, is forced to engage in various sexual acts for money or other forms of payment. This can occur through prostitution, pornography, or any other form of commercial sexual exploitation.

Forced marriage: During a forced marriage, a person, usually a young woman, is forced to marry against their will, usually for the goal of exploitation. In certain polygamous cultures, girls as young as ten and occasionally younger are married to men in their sixties and seventies and forced to be child brides to them.

Child trafficking: Most shocking is that children are trafficked for several purposes. These include forced labor, sexual exploitation, and forced begging. In previous dark times, children would have been intentionally maimed to make people pity them so they could collect more money. Children are particularly vulnerable to trafficking because they are young and lack legal protection.

Organ trafficking: In this gory type of trafficking, a person's organs are taken without consent and sold for transplantation. This tends to happen if there is a long waiting list for organs in hospitals. Wealthy people pay to buy organs on the black market, and innocent people who get into debt are coerced to provide their organs. On a more sinister note, there's been a spate of young people teaching in certain countries in

Southeast Asia who are abducted and never seen again. The rumor mill has it that they've been killed for their organs.

These are just a few examples of the many forms that human trafficking can take. It's a serious crime that violates human rights and affects millions of people around the world.

Fun Fact:

An interesting fact about child brides is that, despite what the first world believes about their impressive laws to protect children, the practice is not restricted to developing countries. In the US, laws vary by state, but in some states, the law allows minors to marry with parental or legal consent. Between 2000 and 2010, more than 200,000 child marriages were in the US.

Fun Fact:

One of the most famous slaves was Joseph; from the Bible, he was sold by his brothers and enslaved in Egypt. He was purchased by Potiphar, who was an officer of Pharaoh. Potiphar's wife attempted to tempt Joseph into bed with her, but as an honorable man, he refused her advances. She had him thrown into prison, where his vivid visions fascinated the guards and eventually won him the trust of Pharaoh, and he became second in charge in the whole of Egypt.

Fill in the blanks to complete the story.

Organ trafficking: In this ___ type of trafficking, a person's organs are taken without consent and sold for ___. This tends to happen if there is a long ____ list for organs in hospitals. Wealthy people pay to buy ____ on the __ market, and innocent people who get into debt are _____ to provide their organs. On a more ______ note, there's been a spate of young people teaching in certain countries in Southeast _____ who are ______ and never seen again. The _____ mill has it that they've been killed for their organs.

Answers:

1. Rumor
2. Abducted
3. Sinister
4. Transportation
5. Coerced
6. Organs
7. Gory
8. Black
9. Waiting
10. Asia

SLAVERY ACROSS THE WORLD

Slavery has existed in one form or another across the World since mankind first learned that they could subjugate people weaker than themselves.

Slavery in Asia

Slavery has occurred in many parts of the world throughout history. The varieties and forms of slavery in Asia differed depending on the time, nation, and culture of the people.

In ancient China, slavery was largely practiced by the ruling classes, and the slaves were people who could not pay their debts. Slaves were commonly prisoners of war or people who had been plunged into debt for one or another reason and sold themselves or their children into slavery to pay off their debts. That must have been a terrifyingly difficult thing to do. China officially abolished slavery during the Qin Dynasty in 221 BC, but unofficially slavery continued in various forms until the 1900s. Interestingly, during the Covid pandemic, people across the world found themselves incarcerated for their "own good," but countries like China were so stringent and controlling in their rules that they enslaved people in their own homes.

In India, several forms of slavery have existed for many thousands of years. These included debt bondage and slavery based on the caste system. The caste system in India is an established hierarchy of social classes. The lowest caste is known as "untouchables," and throughout history, have been given menial or back-breaking jobs and forced to work in slave-like conditions.

In Japan, slavery also occurred in the form of debt bondage. During the Edo period from 1603 to 1868, this was known as "indentured servitude," People who were in debt to powerful landowners or merchants, which could easily happen, were compelled to work off their debts as indentured servants. As you can imagine, winning back their freedom seldom happened in a just period.

Slavery was common throughout Southeast Asia before the arrival of Europeans. Slaves were frequently prisoners of war and were used as servants, laborers, and concubines. Slavery continued in certain parts of Southeast Asia until the 20th century.

Today, slavery is illegal in all countries in Asia. However, various forms of forced labor and human trafficking, particularly in the form of young girls for prostitution, still exist in many places. These practices are frequently tied to destitution, inequality, and a lack of access to education and work opportunities. It's still a terrible problem in Myanmar, where girls are often trafficked into other Asian countries.

Slavery in Africa

Slavery has existed in many forms in most of Africa for centuries. It's usually thought that ruthless colonialists exploited the African content and the people enslaved or subjugated, which is true. Still, slavery was practiced as part of the traditional economic and social systems in African societies, and it took on differing forms, including forced labor, debt bondage, and domestic servitude.

Historically, slavery in Africa was not race or ethnicity-based but was a social construct where individuals from less favored ethnic groups could become slaves. Some people became slaves through capture in conflicts or raids, while others were born into slavery or were enslaved due to outstanding debts or crimes. Often slaves were incorporated into their owners' families and became an integral part of the household.

The dreadful transatlantic slave trade remains one of the biggest blots in world history. It involved the enslavement and forced transportation in horrific conditions of millions of Africans to the Caribbean and the Americas. This was a huge slice of slavery in Africa. European traders bought slaves from African slave traders, including the notorious Kingdom of Dahomey, who were ruthless collectors of slaves from their neighbors. In fact, their whole economy collapsed when Britain abolished slavery.

Today, slavery is illegal in all African countries, although forced labor persists in some areas. Governments, NGOs, and international organizations are all working together to eliminate modern-day slavery and protect the rights of those enslaved in the past. This brings about a new set of challenges in many countries where previously disadvantaged people clash with those whose ancestors had been their oppressors.

Slavery in Europe

Slavery has existed in several forms throughout Europe, dating back to ancient times and continuing into the 1800s.

Slavery was a common practice In ancient Greece and Rome, where slaves were used as soldiers for manual labor and household work. During the Middle Ages, slavery was, by and large, abolished in Western Europe but continued to thrive in Eastern Europe and the Balkan States. Slaves were usually used for agricultural labor, which was cruel and backbreaking work, particularly in the colder parts of Russia.

During the 1400s and some centuries after, the transatlantic slave trade brought huge numbers of enslaved Africans to Europe, where they labored on farms and in mines. Conditions were harsh, and small children would work in the mines as young as three. European countries such as Portugal, Spain, and Britain were important participants in the slave trade, fueled by the need for labor in the Americas.

Slavery in South America.

Slavery was very significant in the history of South America, as in most colonized countries. The European powers took it upon themselves to plunder the raw materials and use and abuse the labor of the indigenous people, who were ill-prepared for the onslaught of weapons and technology. Enslaved Africans were also brought to work on plantations and mines. The conditions under which they labored were harsh, and many died due to overwork, infection, torture, or abuse. Slave rebellions were common in South America, and some enslaved people gained independence.

Although slavery has long been abolished, its legacy impacts the region today. Many Afro-descendant populations in South America face discrimination and marginalization.

Fun Fact:

Spain and Portugal were the two main European powers that established colonies in South America, and both countries relied heavily on slave labor to strengthen their economies. In Brazil (a Portuguese colony), slavery prevailed until 1888. In Colombia, Peru, and Venezuela, slavery was abolished earlier, in the 1800s.

Fun Fact:

Enslaved people were also controlled through the psychological tactics of being told they were inferior to their masters and had no right to resist because they were lesser beings. They were described in certain "scientific" works of the time as being between man and beast.

Complete the Sentence:

1. Enslaved people were controlled by _ _ _ _ _

a) psychological tactics.   b) kind words   c) vicious dogs.

2. South America was largely colonized by _ _ _ _ _.

a) France.   b) England   c) Spain and Portugal.

3. One of the worst periods of the Slave trade was the _ _ _ _ _

a)Transpacific trade   b) Transatlantic trade   c)Black Sea trade.

4. In China, one of the main reasons for slavery was _ _ _ _ _

a)War   b) The Caste system   c)Debt bondage.

5. A fine example of Africans enslaving Africans was _ _ _ _ _.

a)Robert Mugabe   b) The Kingdom of Dahomey   c) South Africans during Apartheid.

Answers:

1. Enslaved people were controlled by _ _ _ _ _

a) psychological tactics.

2. South America was largely colonized by _ _ _ _ _.

c) Spain and Portugal.

3. One of the worst periods of the Slave trade was the _ _ _ _ _

b) Transatlantic trade

4. In China, one of the main reasons for slavery was _ _ _ _ _

c) Debt bondage.

5. A fine example of Africans enslaving Africans was _ _ _ _ _.

b) The Kingdom of Dahomey

SLAVE RESISTANCE AND REBELLION

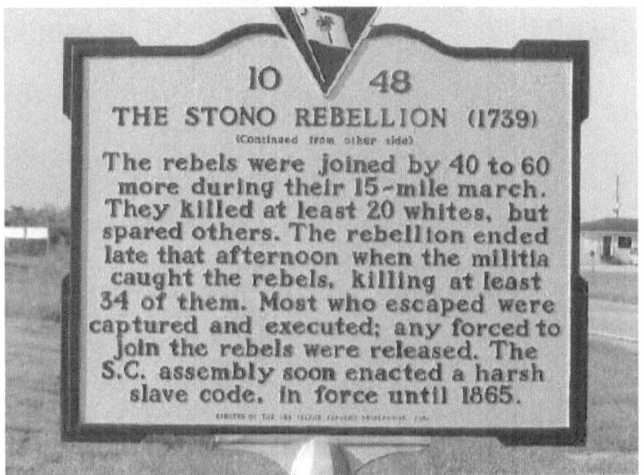

Stono Rebellion: The Stono Rebellion, or Cato's Conspiracy, was a slave rebellion in South Carolina in September 1739. It was the largest slave uprising among the British mainland colonies before the American Revolution.

The uprising was led by a faction of 20 ex-Angolan slaves skilled in rice cultivation. They gathered near the Stono River, 20 miles southwest of Charleston, and started to march south, holding up banners and beating drums. As they traveled, they called other slaves to join them in pursuing freedom.

The Stories of Haiti and Stono and the brave rebellion of Nat Turner

Slave opposition and rebellion related to the various types of resistance enslaved people held against their masters. Slaves were subjected to brutal treatment, forced labor, and several forms of intimidation and oppression. They frequently used resistance when they reached desperation to fight back and regain their freedom.

Slaves exhibited various forms of resistance, from individual resistance, like sabotage and theft, to more systematic forms of resistance, such as uprisings, rebellions, and escape endeavors. These acts of resistance had significant consequences for the slaves and their masters.

Some of the most famous slave rebellions in history include the Haitian Revolution of 1791-1804, led by Toussaint L'Ouverture, the Nat Turner Rebellion in 1831 in Virginia, and the Stono Rebellion in 1739 in South Carolina.

In these cases, brave people could no longer endure suffering and injustice and fought to free themselves.

Haiti's Slave Wars.

The Slave Wars in Haiti were a sequel of rebellions and uprisings led by enslaved Afro-Caribbean and Africans against the French colonial government and the slave owners in Haiti (Saint-Domingue).

In August 1791, the first significant Slave War in Haiti began when enslaved people revolted against their overlords and attacked plantations across the island. This rebellion spread like wildfire and became a full-scale rebellion lasting more than ten years. The leader of this uprising was a former slave Toussaint L'Ouverture, who became a general in the French military and later led the Haitian Revolution.

The Haitian slave war was marked by severe violence and bloodshed on both sides. The French colonial government and slave owners tried to quell the rebellion with vicious force, including large-scale executions, torture, and other horrors. In response, the slave armies fought back, drove the French out of Haiti, and established the world's first autonomous black republic. This was a turning point in world history

Nat Turner's Rebellion

This was a slave rebellion in Southampton County, Virginia, in August 1831, led by Nat Turner, a slave preacher who believed that God had chosen him to lead his people out of slavery. Turner and a significantly small group of fellow slaves murdered about 60 white men, women, and children before the state militia put down the rebellion.

The rebellion helped fuel the abolitionist movement in the United States and create awareness even though Nat Turner was apprehended two months after the rebellion and was tried, convicted, and executed. His rebellion opened doors for future freedom.

Stono Rebellion

The Stono Rebellion, or Cato's Conspiracy, was a slave rebellion in South Carolina in September 1739. It was the largest slave uprising among the British mainland colonies before the American Revolution.

The uprising was led by a faction of 20 ex-Angolan slaves skilled in rice cultivation. They gathered near the Stono River, 20 miles southwest of Charleston, and started to march south, holding up banners and beating drums. As they traveled, they called other slaves to join them in pursuing freedom.

They invaded several ranches, killing about 20 white people and burning several buildings. They also collected weapons and bullets as they went. However, as they led the way toward Spanish Florida and potential freedom, they were confronted by a militia. A battle arose, and many were killed, apprehended, or had to flee.

As a consequence of the rebellion, the South Carolina congress passed a series of cruel laws restricting the movement and behavior of slaves. The Negro Act of 1740 included conditions that made it criminal for slaves to gather, grow their own food, make money, or learn to read and write. The act also required all white men to carry firearms to church on Sundays to deter future uprisings.

The Stono Rebellion was significant by demonstrating the conditions that slaves faced. It also illustrated the determination of slaves to fight for their independence, even at the risk of their lives.

Fun Fact:

The Nat Turner rebellion created genuine terror in the slave owners. It led to waves of panic and hatred among white slaveholders, who worried that other slaves would arise against them. As a result, there were extensive killings of slaves, most of whom had nothing to do with the rebellion.

Fun Fact:

The Haitian Revolution challenged the world order of the time. The global community endorsed European colonialism and the myth of white supremacy. The Haitian Revolution encouraged other anti-colonial movements and contributed to the dissolution of slavery throughout the Americas.

Discussion Point.

If the slave owners had been less harsh when suppressing revolutions and offered a few human rights concessions, do you think enslaved people might have settled down to their lots, and slavery might have continued for longer? **Justify your response.**

THE THIRD SERVILE WAR – ONE OF THE GREATEST SLAVE REVOLTS

The Third Servile War: The Third Servile War occurred between 73-71 BC. This was made famous by the rebellious slave Spartacus. Spartacus led a dramatic, albeit unsuccessful rebellion against Rome, known as the Gladiator War

Spartacus, the commander of the Third Servile War, was popularly known as the Gladiator Warrior. Spartacus was a gladiator and leader of a slave uprising against the Roman Republic in the late 1st century BCE. He was born in Thrace, modern-day Bulgaria, and was captured by the Romans and sold into slavery.

This significant uprising took place in ancient Rome from 73-71 BC. A group of slaves fought the war. They were mainly gladiators trained in desperate combat who rebelled against their Roman overlords and strived to achieve their freedom. Spartacus was one of the main leaders of the uprising and is known by history for his military skill, leadership abilities, and courage in fighting for the rights of other slaves. They eventually amassed a regiment of over 100,000 men and marched north toward the Alps, intending to escape to freedom.

Spartacus had initially escaped from a gladiatorial training school in Capua with around 70 other gladiators. They took refuge on the famous volcano Mount Vesuvius, where other slaves joined them, attracted by the prospect of independence and revenge against their overlords. Gladiator schools, also known as "Ludi," were training schools where gladiators were equipped to excel in combat techniques, endurance, and physical fitness. These schools were normally run by a "lanista," the gladiators' manager.

The training regimen in a gladiator school was fierce and

tough, as gladiators had to be in top physical condition to battle in the arena. Gladiators were trained in various combat styles and weapons, including spears, swords, shields, and nets. They learned how to fight in various formations and against numerous opponents. As one can see, they were ideally qualified to lead a battle.

Spartacus proved to be a dynamic and effective commander, and he organized his supporters into a formidable force that overthrew several Roman armies sent against them. The rebels won remarkable victories, and at the peak of their struggle, they controlled most of southern Italy.

Despite initial successes, the Roman regiments eventually crushed the uprising, and Spartacus was killed in the final battle by the Roman general Marcus Licinius Crassus in 71 BC. The slaves that survived were unfortunate because the Romans crucified them along the Appian Way. This was a famous Roman road leading from Rome to southern Italy. This terrible death of being nailed to a wooden cross and left to die in excruciating agony and thirst was a harsh warning to others contemplating rebelling against the Republic.

Spartacus has become a symbol of resistance against oppression and has been the subject of numerous books, movies, and TV shows. His story has been interpreted in various ways over time, but he is generally remembered as a courageous leader who fought for freedom and justice for himself and his fellow slaves.

Despite their ultimate defeat, the rebels were able to motivate and enthrall future generations of slaves and oppressed people. The story of Spartacus has continued as a lasting symbol of resistance and freedom.

Fun Fact:

There were vast numbers of slaves traded throughout the Roman empire, from Britain in the North to Syria in the East. At the beginning of the Imperial age, it is thought that the ratio of slaves to freeborn people in Rome was 3:1. It seems obvious that a disparity like that would have eventually led to rebellion.

Fun Fact:

The Servile Wars were important in the history of ancient Rome, as they indicated the tensions between the enslaved populations and the free citizens. These rebellions showed that slaves were able and willing to organize and lead successful uprisings and that the Roman Republic was susceptible to internal turmoil.

Fill in the missing words:

The Second -1- War, also known as the Slave War of Sicily, took place in ancient -2- from 104-100 BCE. The rebellion was led by a slave named -3-, who managed to unite a diverse group of slaves, including -4- laborers and miners, in a bid to overthrow their Roman masters. The rebellion was initially -5-, and the slaves managed to seize -6- of large parts of the island of -7-. However, the Romans eventually rallied and, with the help of local -8-, were able to -9- the rebellion and reassert control over the island. Athenian was captured and -10-, along with many of his followers

Answers:

1. Servile
2. Rome
3. Athenian
4. Agricultural
5. Successful
6. Seize
7. Sicily
8. Allies
9. Crush
10. Executed

SOME UNUSUAL CASES OF SLAVE WARS

The Flying Dutchman: There is a famous legend of the "Flying Dutchman," which is said to be a ghost ship cursed to sail the seas forever. According to this legend, the Flying Dutchman was a slave ship carrying a cargo of enslaved people when it met a severe storm off the coast of South Africa. The ship floundered, and all the enslaved people on board died. The ship's captain apparently cursed the vessel to sail the seas forever as retribution for failing to deliver his slave cargo to its destination.

Not all Slave wars had a happy ending with the enslaved people winning their freedom or a more usual tragic ending in capture and death. The two Slave Wars we will examine next had very strange and different endings.

The Amistad Rebellion

The Amistad Rebellion was a famous occurrence in 1839

when a group of African slaves rebelled against their captors on board the Spanish slave ship La Amistad. Slave ships were terrible places full of suffering, overcrowding, and human misery. Many slaves died from disease, overcrowding, and starvation en route to the New World. This ship was transferring captives from Havana, Cuba, to the Spanish colony of Puerto Principe, now called Camagüey, Cuba. This was when the rebellion happened.

The leader of the uprising was Sengbe Pieh, also called Joseph Cinqué. It was common to rename slaves to make recalling their names easier. Sengbe Pieh had been caught in present-day Sierra Leone and sold into slavery. With his fellow captives, they were able to overwhelm the crew of the Amistad and take custody of the ship. They endeavored to sail back to Africa but were apprehended by the US Navy just off the coast of Long Island, New York.

The enslaved Africans were thereafter detained, and a legal battle took place over their fate. The Spanish government contended that the captives were their property and insisted on their return, while slave abolitionists argued that the Africans had been abducted and had the right to freedom.

The case went to the US Supreme Court, where it was contested for the slaves by former President John Quincy Adams. In a landmark judgment, the judge ruled that the Africans had been illegally seized from their country and were entitled to be free. The enslaved Africans finally returned to their home country of Sierra Leone with the assistance of various abolitionist organizations.

The Amistad Rebellion became a symbol of the battle against slavery and was seen as a substantial accomplishment for the abolitionist movement.

Igbo Landing

This refers to an event that happened in 1803 on St. Simons Island, Georgia, in which a faction of Igbo slaves who had been newly enslaved from Nigeria and brought to the island revolted and elected to walk into the water and drown themselves rather than be enslaved in the Americas.

There are several accounts of the event, and its precise details remain debated among historians. Nonetheless, it is widely upheld that the Igbo Landing is a significant moment in the narrative of the transatlantic slave trade and an influential symbol of opposition to enslavement. Today, the area is celebrated with a historical marker and is perceived as a significant site for studying African-American history.

Over and over again, the strong indomitable human spirit shows that people would go to any length to free themselves once their quality of life no longer sustains any hope for the future. Even death is better than oppression.

Fun Fact:

Legend has it that the Igbo people chose to perish by drowning themselves because they concluded, based on their traditional beliefs, they would return to their country after death. Today, the Igbo Landing site is sacred for many African Americans and is frequently visited by those wishing to honor the memory of the brave Igbo people.

Fun Fact:

There is a famous legend of the "Flying Dutchman," which is said to be a ghost ship cursed to sail the seas forever. According to this legend, the Flying Dutchman was a slave ship carrying a cargo of enslaved people when it met a severe storm off the coast of South Africa. The ship floundered, and all the enslaved people on board died. The ship's captain apparently cursed the vessel to sail the seas forever as retribution for failing to deliver his slave cargo to its destination.

True or False Amistad Rebellion Facts:

1. True or False. The Amistad Rebellion occurred on a ship carrying slaves from the Caribbean to the US.

2. True or False. The rebellion started when the slaves overwhelmed the ship's crew and endeavored to sail back to Africa.

3. True or False The ship was ultimately stopped by the U.S. Navy vessel off the coast of Long Island, New York.

4. True or False. The U.S. government originally allowed the Spanish government to try the slaves for mutiny and pirating.

5. True or False. The slaves were ultimately freed after a legal crusade that went all the way to the U.S. Supreme Court.

6. True or False. John Quincy Adams was a lawyer who argued on behalf of the slaves in the Supreme Court.

7. True or False. The Supreme Court ruled that the slaves were free and should be returned to their home country of Sierra Leone.

8. True or False. The Amistad rebellion was a crucial moment in the abolitionist movement in the US.

Answers:

1. True

2. True

3. False. The ship was stopped off the coast of Long Island, New York, by a U.S. Revenue Ship.

4. True

5. True

6. True

7. False. The Supreme Court ruled that the slaves were free and should be permitted to return to Africa if they wished, but they were not ordered to return to Sierra Leone should they not wish to go.

8. True

ABOLITION OF SLAVERY

Finally, people became enlightened to the fact that enslaving other human beings was a cruel and terrible thing to do. Of course, not everyone thinks like this, as people can justify anything. So it took a long time and a lot of change in thinking for slavery to be abolished finally. As we have discussed, slavery still exists in various forms, and none of them are legal today.

The reasons slavery was abolished varied. The moral reasoning came from abolitionists and religious groups, who believed slavery was morally wrong and violated the basic human rights of enslaved individuals.

Economic reasoning also held sway. With the growth in industrialization beginning to take hold in the 1800s, the economic benefits of slavery became less important. A system of slavery became expensive to maintain.

A major political reason in the US was the conflict between

the Northern and Southern States of America, which led to the American Civil War. When the Unionists won, it meant the end of slavery. The 13th Amendment abolished it for good.

The Social reasons for the abolition of slavery were driven by changing social attitudes toward race and equality. Many people began to realize that slavery was a form of racism perpetuating inequality and injustice.

The movement to abolish slavery gained momentum in the 1700s and 1800s, particularly in Europe and North America. They also argued that slavery was economically ineffective and hindered growth in societies that practiced it.

The abolition of slavery was a lengthy and difficult struggle that involved political and social activism. In many cases, abolitionists faced harsh resistance from slave owners and their supporters. However, through the efforts of many people and institutions, slavery was eventually repealed in many parts of the world.

Abolition of slavery in America

The abolition of slavery in America was a long and complex

process that took place over several decades, beginning with the American Revolution and culminating in the passage of the 13th Amendment to the United States Constitution in 1865.

The American Civil War from 1861-1865 played a significant role in the abolition of slavery. The war started as a dispute over states' rights and expanding territory, but it was soon obvious that the main issue was slavery. President Abraham Lincoln published the Emancipation Proclamation in 1863, which announced that all slaves in Confederate-held territory were to be given their freedom. One can just imagine the stir that caused. Although the proclamation did not instantly free all slaves, it was a meaningful step toward the eventual dissolution of slavery in America.

The 13th Amendment to the United States Constitution, approved in 1865, officially abolished slavery. This was a key moment in American history. However, the legacy of slavery continued to have a major impact on American society, and it took much longer for African Americans to be treated as American citizens with equal rights.

Abolition of slavery in Europe

This was a slow process that took place over several centuries, with different regions and countries enforcing their laws and agreements to end slavery.

In the Middle Ages, slavery was common in much of Europe, particularly in southern Europe, where Muslim slave traders brought prisoners from Africa and the Middle East to be peddled in the slave markets of Venice and Genoa. By the 14th century, slavery had largely vanished in northern Europe, and more centralized forms of government had taken over feudalism.

In the modern age, the movement to repeal slavery gained impetus in the late 1700s as Enlightenment notions about human rights and dignity began to spread throughout Europe. In 1807, Britain passed the Abolition of the Slave Trade Act. This banned the dreadful transatlantic slave trade. In 1833, it passed the Slavery Abolition Act, which repealed slavery throughout the British Empire. Other European countries followed suit, with France abolishing slavery in its colonies in 1848 and the Netherlands in 1863.

Fun Fact:

The abolitionist movement in America gained much support with the publication of Harriet Beecher Stowe's novel "Uncle Tom's Cabin" in 1852. This disturbing yet touching novel portrayed the brutal truths of slavery and helped to galvanize public opinion against the institution. It's worth reading just to look at slavery through the eyes of a writer from the 1800s.

Fun Fact:

Russia officially abolished slavery in 1861, under the reign of Tsar Alexander II. Russian slavery was called serfdom, and it existed in Russia for centuries. The peasants were tied to the land in the service of the noble landlords who owned it. They were not permitted to leave their land without permission and provided forced labor for their landlords.

Discussion Question:

What were the major factors that led to the abolition of slavery, and how did the abolition of slavery impact the social, economic, and political landscape of the countries where it occurred? You might have to do a bit more reading for this one. Some useful references are.

The American Civil War Museum's "The Fight for Freedom: Emancipation and Abolition" resource page: Provides access to the primary source material and videos related to the abolition of slavery in the United States.

The International Slavery Museum's Abolition resource page: This page provides information on the history of slavery and its abolition, focusing on the British abolition movement.

THE DIFFERENT FACES OF SLAVERY

Apartheid: Apartheid was a system of institutionalized racial segregation and intolerance enforced by the South African government from 1948 to 1994. The system denied basic rights and freedoms to black South Africans and instituted a system of systemic racial inequality. The word "apartheid" is derived from the Afrikaans language and means "separateness" or "apartness.

Even though slavery, as in the right to own a human being, has disappeared, oppression is still alive. This is a systemic practice of racism, discrimination, exploitation, and marginalization that targets certain people or groups based on their race, beliefs, or culture.

Here are some examples, some of which are still common in parts of the world today. Others, fortunately, have disappeared, but their legacy remains.

Forced labor: Forced labor is a type of modern-day slavery that forces people to work without pay, on ridiculously low wages, or under threat of violence. This practice still prevails in many industries of the world, particularly agriculture, mining, and manufacturing.

Bonded labor is a form of modern-day slavery where people are compelled to work to repay a debt or loan, which is often inflated, and the workers end up working for years or even their whole lives to repay **them.**

Child labor is when children are compelled to work instead of going to school or playing. It is a form of slavery because they are often forced to work in hazardous and exploitative circumstances.

Domestic servitude is when people are forced to work in private homes as domestic workers. They are often isolated, have no access to the outside world, and are subjected to emotional and physical abuse.

As discussed earlier, **human trafficking** is still a global scourge. Human trafficking involves recruiting, transporting, and exploiting individuals for forced labor or sexual exploitation.

The **Jim Crow laws** were a system of legal segregation and discrimination against African Americans in the United States, lasting from the late 1800s to the mid-1960s. These nefarious laws restricted African Americans' access to equal education, housing, jobs, and public transport and perpetuated racial inequality.

Apartheid was a system of institutionalized racial segregation and intolerance enforced by the South African government from 1948 to 1994. The system denied basic rights and freedoms to black South Africans and instituted a system of systemic racial inequality. The word "apartheid" is derived from the Afrikaans language and means "separateness" or "apartness."

Under the apartheid system, South African society was divided into four main racial groups, White, Black, Coloured, and Indian. The government used laws and policies to enforce racial segregation and withhold basic human rights from Black South Africans, who comprised most of the population.

Some key characteristics of apartheid included the

mandatory removal of millions of Black South Africans from their homes and the development of "homelands" or Bantustans, which were distinct and unequal areas established for Black people. The government also imposed stringent pass laws that limited the movement of Black people and restricted their access to education and healthcare.

The **Caste system** is the hierarchical social structure that still exists in places like India, Nepal, and Sri Lanka. These systems assign people to a specific social position based on birth and constrain their opportunities and freedoms based on caste.

All these features of oppression involve the organized and institutionalized rejection of basic human rights and freedoms to certain people or groups of people. The results of this haunt society for generations afterward.

Fun Fact:

During deep Apartheid in the 1960s, black domestic workers lived in rooms outside the homes of their white employers. They were not allowed to have a husband in the room with them, and if a child was born, he or she had to be sent back to the homeland to live with the family when only a few months old, effectively separating mother and child.

Fun Fact:

Some of the most prominent rebels against Jim Crow laws were civil rights activists such as Martin Luther King Jr and Rosa Parks. They used nonviolent resistance and civil disobedience to question the laws and bring awareness to the issue of racial inequality. It's fascinating to find out more about their lives.

Circle the correct word:

1. The Caste system occurs in

a)India   b) South Africa.

2. The systemic oppression in South Africa was called

a) Apartheid   b) Separate Development.

3. When a person works to pay back a debt, it's called

a) forced labor   b) bonded labor

4. A rebel against the Jim Crow laws was

a) Nelson Mandela   b) Martin Luther King Jr

5. South African black people were forced to live in homelands called

a) Bantustans   b) Khayas

6. The four groups of people identified to live apart in South Africa were White, Black, Coloured and

a) Indian   b) Chinese

7. The language of oppression in South Africa was

a) Zulu   b)Afrikaans

8. Forced labor is most common in mining, manufacturing, and

a) agriculture   b) fisheries

Answers:

1. India
2. Apartheid
3. Bonded labor
4. Martin Luther King Jr.
5. Bantustans
6. Indian
7. Afrikaans
8. Agriculture

MODERN DAY MOVEMENTS AGAINST SYSTEMIC OPPRESSION.

Wokeness: Of course, there are always people who take everything a touch too far. We are all familiar with the term "wokeness," commonly used to describe a social and political movement that intends to raise awareness and nurture progressive values related to issues like social justice, inequality, and discrimination. This is obviously a good thing, but certain extreme and radical groups may align themselves with the wokeness movement and discriminate against or abide by people they consider non-woke.

In a world that seems obsessed with economic gain and greed, it's good to realize that some people act against oppression. Many modern-day movements against systemic oppression are active throughout the world. Some of the most prominent ones include:

The **Black Lives Matter (BLM)** movement is an international movement that crusades against violence and systemic racism toward Black people. The movement recently gained impetus after the death of George Floyd, violently killed by police officers in Minneapolis in 2020. The movement has been involved in various uprisings, political rallies, and advocacy actions.

The #**MeToo** movement began as a hashtag on social media in 2017, aiming to bring attention to sexual harassment and rape. The movement aims to empower survivors and hold the perpetrators to account for their actions.

The LGBTQ+ rights movement has been active for many years but has increased significant momentum recently. The movement supports equal rights and protection for people who identify as lesbian, gay, bisexual, transgender, queer, or questioning.

The **climate justice** movement intends to address the disproportionate consequences of climate change on marginalized communities. The movement supports policies and actions prioritizing the needs of those most impacted by climate change, including low-income populations and colored communities.

Indigenous rights movements strive to address the ongoing consequences of colonization, genocide, and systemic discrimination against Indigenous peoples. These movements aim to facilitate recognizing and preserving Indigenous societies, territories, and independence.

Disability rights movements support equal rights and chances for people with disabilities. These movements aim to deal with systemic discrimination and obstacles to the accessibility of disabled people in areas such as healthcare, education, and employment.

These are a few examples of modern-day movements against systemic oppression. Each movement has its personal history, goals, and policies, but all share the goal of questioning and shifting systemic oppression and inequality.

"Wokeness" The Flip Side?

Of course, some people always take everything a touch too far. We are all familiar with the term "wokeness," commonly used to describe a social and political movement that intends to raise awareness and nurture progressive values related to issues like social justice, inequality, and discrimination. This is obviously a good thing, but certain extreme and radical groups may align themselves with the wokeness movement and discriminate against or abide by people they consider non-woke.

Extreme Wokeness Examples.

Some examples of actions or beliefs that some people might consider "extreme wokeness" are:

They demand that all books and movies with offensive content be banned or censored. An example of this can be seen in our Interesting Fact.

Believing that all representations of inequality or racism are intentional and must be punished.

Refusing to engage with people with differing views or opinions, labeling them ignorant or bigoted.

Insisting on using gender-neutral pronouns in all contexts, even when it goes against the individual's preferred pronouns.

Using social media to publicly insult and shame people who make a mistake or say something deemed offensive without giving them a chance to learn and grow from their mistake.

It really seems that some people can never find a balance!

Fun Fact:

An example of extreme wokeness recently hit our news headlines when sensitivity editors were called in to remove all offensive words from the famous Roald Dahl books. The disgusting glutton Augustus Gloop was no longer allowed to be called fat, but the silliest example was removing all reference to color so that a black cloak became just a cloak. I don't think fabric can be racist. Do you?

Fun Fact:

LGBTQ+ rights movements and organizations have battled against anti-discrimination laws, marriage equality, and the repeal of sodomy laws. They have also challenged patriarchal structures and gender roles within the LGBTQ+ community and broader society.

True or False Discussion Questions:

There are no 100% right or wrong answers here, but please justify your responses.

1. "Wokeness" refers to a political or social doctrine that emphasizes understanding issues related to social justice and inequality. **True or False?**

2. The term "woke" originates in African American Vernacular English (AAVE) and was initially used to describe a state of awareness of racial injustice and racism. **True or False?**

3. The concept of wokeness is primarily concerned with identity politics and concentrates on issues about race, gender, and sexuality. **True or False?**

4. Critics of wokeness argue that it prioritizes individual identity and not shared experiences and common objectives. **True or False?**

5. The term "cancel culture" is associated with wokeness and refers to rejecting or boycotting people or bodies that are thought to have infringed social norms or values. **True or False?**

6. Supporters of wokeness believe that dealing with systemic issues of oppression and inequality is essential to establish a more just and impartial society. **True or False?**

7. Wokeness is often associated with political correctness, which refers to avoiding language or actions that could be discerned as marginalizing. **True or False?**

8. The term "anti-woke" describes people who reject the beliefs of wokeness and see it as a threat to freedom of speech and academic diversity. **True or False?**

CONCLUSION

"Freedom is never given; it is won."

– A. Philip Randolph

Although slavery is a fundamental abuse of human rights and a grim injustice that has resulted in immense misery for millions of enslaved people throughout human history, the wars fought by enslaved people have aided humanity. While it is impossible to rationalize or idealize violence, some positive impacts have resulted from these wars.

One of the important ways the slave wars have aided humanity is by questioning the systems of oppression that enabled slavery to occur. The fight for independence and autonomy by the enslaved people throughout history was an influential force inspiring other enslaved groups to take courage and defend their rights to freedom. The Haitian Revolution is a great example of this, as it was the first triumphant slave rebellion in modern history, leading the first autonomous Black nation in the world. This uprising had a ripple effect across the Atlantic, motivating other enslaved peoples to struggle for their independence and eventually ending slavery across many parts of the world.

Another likely benefit of slave wars is how they uncovered the harsh realities of enslavement to the world. The descriptions of enslaved peoples who rebelled against their oppressors indicated the horrific cruelty and injustice on sugar and cotton plantations. These tales, often communicated through oral traditions or written reports by abolitionists, assisted in galvanizing public opinion against slavery and pushing for its abolition.

While one cannot talk conclusively about the benefits of slave wars because of the horrifying loss and trauma created, we can make these points. Slave wars exposed the brutality of the establishment. Slave wars led to eventual freedom. Slave Wars provided models for survival and independence and contributed to the struggle for justice and equality.

BIBLIOGRAPHY

- Slavery | Definition, History, & Facts | Britannica. Staff Writer. Updated February 2023.

  https://www.britannica.com/topic/slavery-sociology

- A Brief History of Civil Rights in the United States: The Black Lives Matter Movement.Staff Writer. Updated February 2023.

  https://library.law.howard.edu/civilrightshistory/BLM #:~:text=In%202013%2C%20three%20female%20Black, project%20called%20Black%20Lives%20Matter.

- What is forced labor, modern slavery, and human trafficking. Staff Writer. Updated December 2022

  https://www.ilo.org/global/topics/forced-labour/ definition/lang--en/index.htm#:~:text=The%20Definition %20of%20forced%20labour&text=%22all%20work%20or% 20service%20which,offered%20himself%20or%20herself% 20voluntarily.%2

- The Five Greatest Slave Rebellions in the United States | African American History Blog | The African Americans: Many Rivers to Cross. Henry Louise Gates. Updated October 2022.

  https://www.pbs.org/wnet/african-americans-many-rivers-to- cross/history/did-african-american-slaves-rebel

- 7 Famous Slave Revolts - HISTORY. Evan Andrews. Updated April 2021.

  https://www.history.com/news/7-famous-slave-revolts

- Slave rebellions | History, Examples, & Facts | Britannica.Staff Writer. Updated February 2023.

https://www.britannica.com/topic/slave-rebellions

- What does woke mean? Definition of woke culture in 2023 - and what critics mean by 'woke police'. Rhona Shennan 30th January 2023.
  https://www.nationalworld.com/whats-on/arts-and-entertainment/what-does-woke-mean-definition-woke-culture-2023-3215758.

Image License-Free

- **Chapter 5:** The Third Servile War: The Third Servile War occurred between 73-71 BC. This was made famous by the rebellious slave Spartacus. Spartacus led a dramatic, albeit unsuccessful rebellion against Rome, known as the Gladiator War. https://en.wikipedia.org/wiki/File:Tod_des_Spartacus_by_Hermann_Vogel.jpg

- **Chapter 1:** The Zanj Rebellion: The Zanj Rebellion of 869-883 AD. This major uprising in Iraq against the Arab Abbasid Caliphate by enslaved Africans. The Zanj (Tanzanian) slaves revolted against their Arab rulers, led by Ali bin Muhammad. They succeeded in capturing the city of Basra and other big towns, and formed their own nation, called the "State of the Blacks." In the end, they were defeated but they had ten successful years of freedom. https://en.wikipedia.org/wiki/Zanj_Rebellion#/media/File:Zanj_Rebellion.svg

- **Chapter 4:** Stono Rebellion: The Stono Rebellion, or Cato's Conspiracy, was a slave rebellion in South Carolina in September 1739. It was the largest slave uprising among the British mainland colonies before the American Revolution. The uprising was led by a faction of 20 ex-Angolan slaves skilled in rice cultivation. They gathered near the Stono River, 20 miles southwest of Charleston, and started to march south, holding up banners and beating drums. As they traveled, they called other slaves to join them in pursuing freedom.

https://www.flickr.com/photos/hdescopeland/3779530279

- **Chapter 6:** The Flying Dutchman: There is a famous legend of the "Flying Dutchman," which is said to be a ghost ship cursed to sail the seas forever. According to this legend, the Flying Dutchman was a slave ship carrying a cargo of enslaved people when it met a severe storm off the coast of South Africa. The ship floundered, and all the enslaved people on board died. The ship's captain apparently cursed the vessel to sail the seas forever as retribution for failing to deliver his slave cargo to its destination.

https://en.wikipedia.org/wiki/Flying_Dutchman#/media/File:Flying_Dutchman,_the.jpg

- **Chapter 8:** Apartheid: Apartheid was a system of institutionalized racial segregation and intolerance enforced by the South African government from 1948 to 1994. The system denied basic rights and freedoms to black South Africans and instituted a system of systemic racial inequality. The word "apartheid" is derived from the Afrikaans language and means "separateness" or "apartness."

https://en.wikipedia.org/wiki/File:DurbanSign1989.jpg

- **Chapter 7:** The American Civil War: The American Civil War from 1861-1865 played a significant role in the abolition of slavery. The war started as a dispute over states' rights and expanding territory, but it was soon obvious that the main issue was slavery. President Abraham Lincoln published the Emancipation Proclamation in 1863, which announced that all slaves in Confederate-held territory were to be given their freedom. One can just imagine the stir that caused. Although the proclamation did not instantly free all slaves, it was a meaningful step toward the eventual dissolution of slavery in America.

  https://en.wikipedia.org/wiki/Battle_of_Gettysburg

- **Chapter 10:** Wokeness: Of course, there are always people who take everything a touch too far. We are all familiar with the term "wokeness," commonly used to describe a social and political movement that intends to raise awareness and nurture progressive values related to issues like social justice, inequality, and discrimination. This is obviously a good thing, but certain extreme and radical groups may align themselves with the wokeness movement and discriminate against or abide by people they consider non-woke. https://en.wikipedia.org/wiki/Woke#/media/File:Marcia_Fudge_with_Stay_Woke_Vote_t-shirt_in_2018.jpg

About Us

At our core, we believe that history is more than just a subject to be learned. It's an experience to be had.

Our mission is to educate and inspire the next generation by providing them with a window into the fascinating and often surprising world of the past. We want to help young people make sense of the complexities of history and understand the lessons it has to offer.

By creating unforgettable encounters with relics of the past, we hope to ignite a lifelong passion for learning and discovery.

Thank you,

www.ingramcontent.com/pod-product-compliance
Lightning Source LLC
Chambersburg PA
CBHW031319130726
47988CB00007B/2889